SMART BRAIN RIGHT BRAIN

An Introduction to Fractions

Om KIDZ
An imprint of Om Books International

Om Kidz | Om Books International

Reprinted in 2023

Corporate & Editorial Office
A-12, Sector 64, Noida 201 301
Uttar Pradesh, India
Phone: +91 120 477 4100
Email: editorial@ombooks.com
Website: www.ombooksinternational.com

Sales Office
107, Ansari Road, Darya Ganj
New Delhi 110 002, India
Phone: +91 11 4000 9000
Email: sales@ombooks.com

Author: Shweta Sinha
Editor: Kirti Pathak
Art & Design: Anshuman Pandey, Gaurav Bhandari, Harish Arya

ISBN: 978-93-52768-56-1

Printed in India

10 9 8 7 6 5 4 3 2

CONTENTS

1. What Are Fractions?

Mario had a bar of chocolate. His mother asked him to share it with his little sister, Ana. Mario broke up the bar into two equal parts.

One of two parts of a whole chocolate bar.

After sharing the chocolate with Ana, Mario now has one of two parts.

DID YOU KNOW?

The word fraction comes from the Latin word **'fractio'** which means to break.

Let's do some counting. Mario and Ana made sandwiches. How many sandwiches did they make?

They made 3 sandwiches. After eating 2 sandwiches, they decided to share the third one. But, how can you count parts of a sandwich?

One whole sandwich is divided between the two of them. These are only a **part of a whole**.

Of the third sandwich, Ana and Mario each have 1 of 2 parts of the whole sandwich. To count parts of a whole, you need to use **fractions**.

POCKET FACT

When you divide something into equal parts, you get fractions.

When you break something into a number of equal parts, a fraction tells you how many parts you have.

Mario and Ana ordered a pizza.

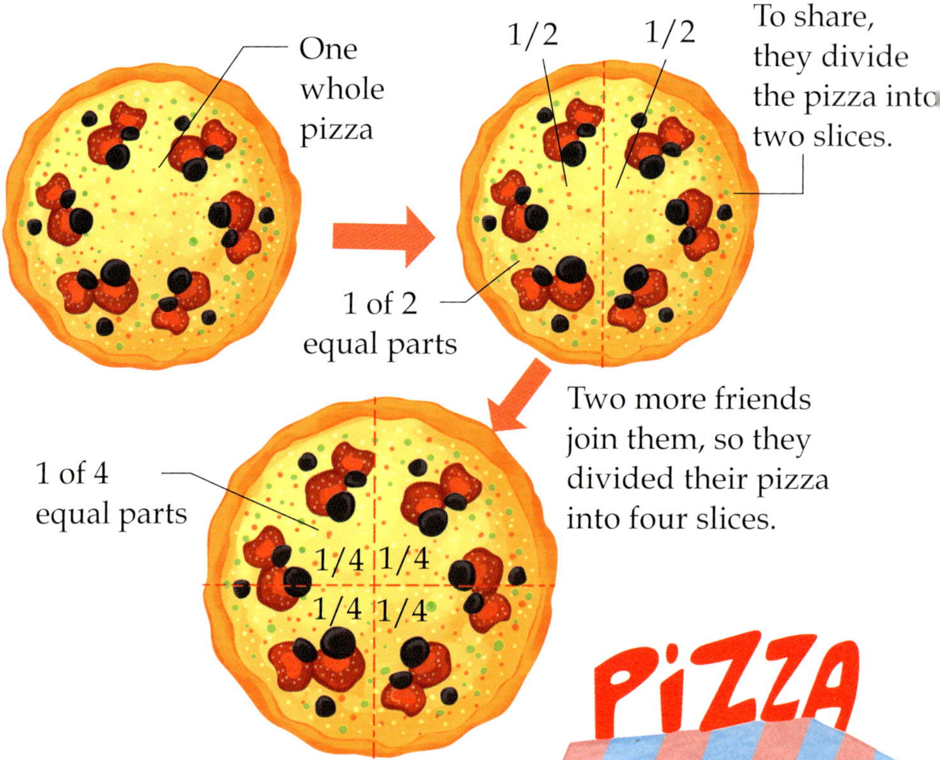

They now have 4 parts of one whole pizza.

POCKET FACT

Fractions were first used by the Egyptians during the era of the pharaohs.

2. Equal Shares

Equal shares are parts of a whole that have the same size or the same value. When Ana and Mario divided their pizza into 2 parts, both parts were equal in size.

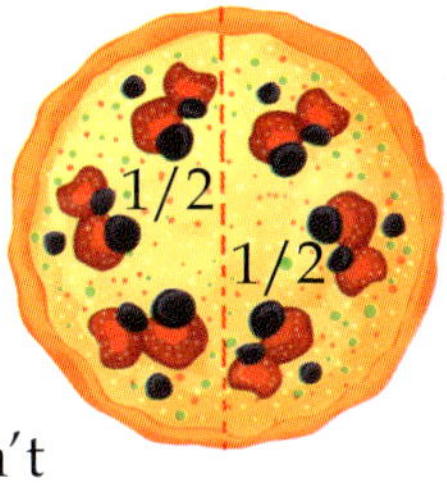

It doesn't matter which direction the pizza is cut to get the two equal parts.

It also doesn't matter if the pizza is a really big one or a small one. As long as the two parts are of equal size, they are equal shares.

Sometimes equal shares may have different shapes.

The water in the bottle and glass have the same size (quantity), but different shapes.

Rectangles divided into 2 equal shares.

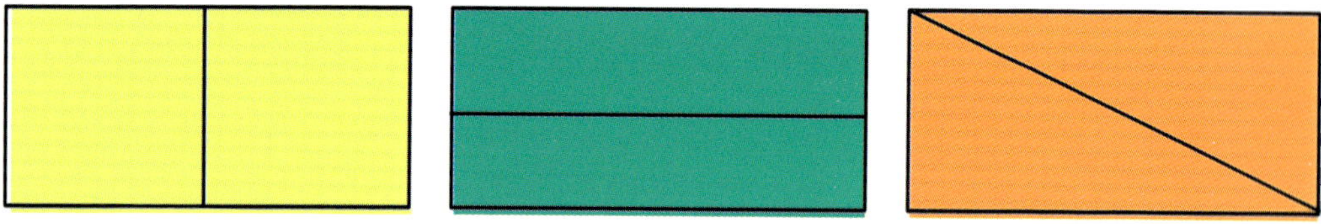

Circles divided into 3 equal shares.

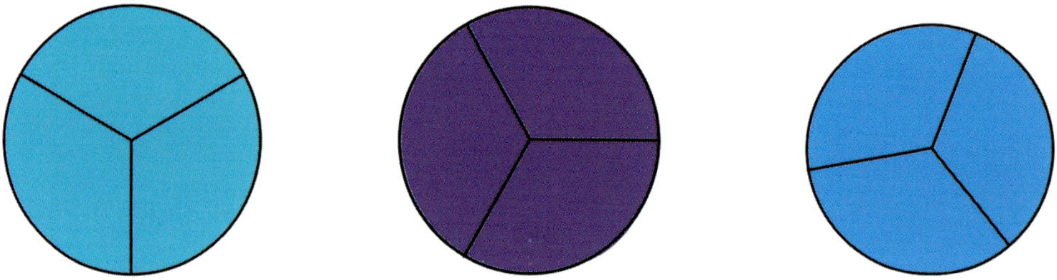

Squares divided into 4 equal shares.

POCKET FACT

Equal shares can be made in multiple ways.

Not a Fraction

It may seem that simply dividing a whole into parts gives us fractions. That is not true. To form fractions, a whole should be divided into **equal shares**.

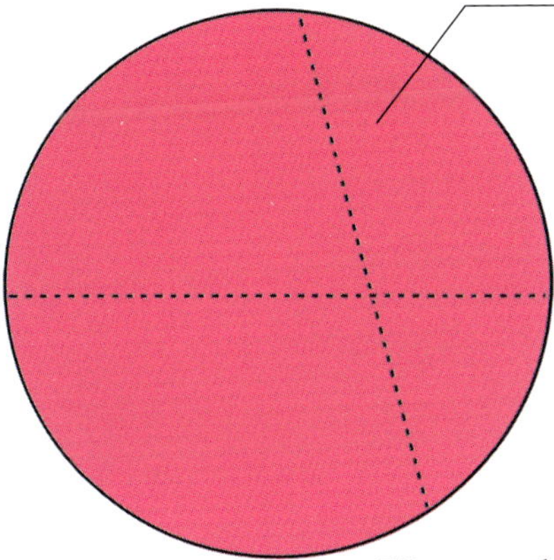

This circle is divided into 4 parts, but the parts are not equal shares. Two parts are larger than the other two parts.

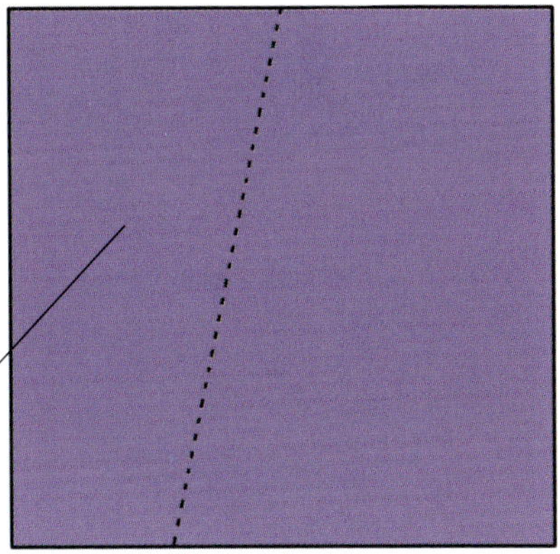

Unequal parts of a square. One part is larger than the other.

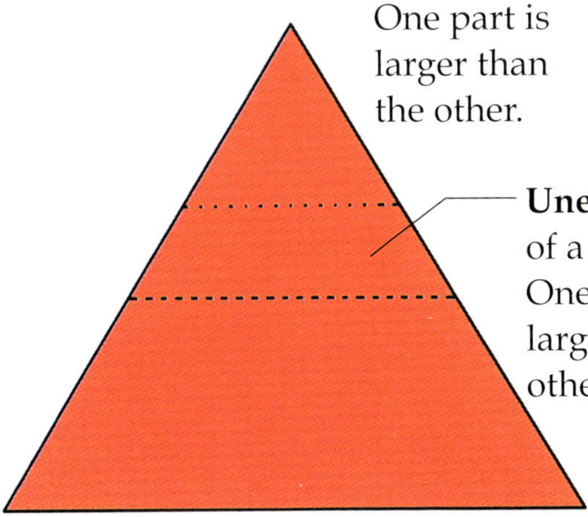

Unequal parts of a triangle. One part is larger than the other two.

POCKET FACT

Unequal parts are not fractions.

Numerator and Denominator

A fraction is written with one number on top and the other number below it.

The number on top is the **Numerator**

A line separates the **numerator** from the **denominator**

Denominator tells you how many equal parts a whole is divided into.

This pizza is divided into 4 equal parts. So, the **denominator** here will be 4.

Numerator tells you how many parts you have.

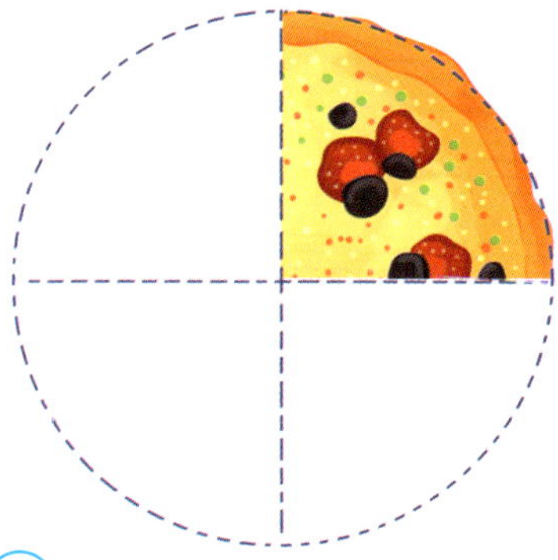

Each person gets 1 slice out of the 4 slices. The numerator indicates how many parts each person has, which is '1'.

Each slice represents 1 part out of 4. So, the fraction that represents each slice is

POCKET FACT

Fractions with the numerator as 1 are called **unit fractions.**

3. Building Fractions

Halves

When you divide a whole into 2 equal parts, you get halves. The fraction for 1 out of 2 parts is 1/2 or a half.

Half of a watermelon

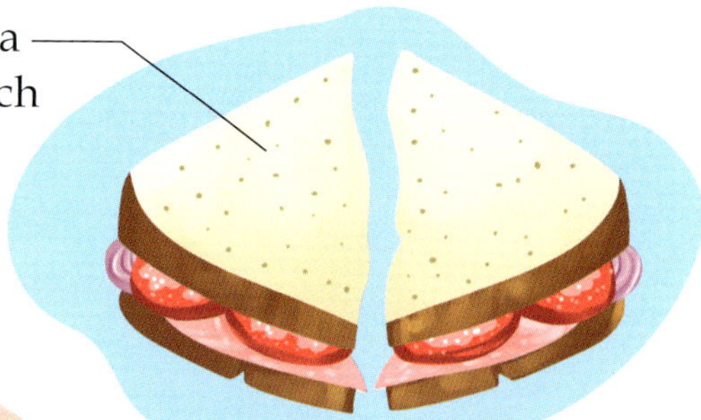

Half of a sandwich

Half of an apple

Half of a triangle

POCKET FACT

Two halves equal one whole.

Quarters

When you divide a whole into 4 equal parts, you get quarters. The fraction for 1 out of 4 parts is 1/4 or a quarter.

A quarter of a rectangle

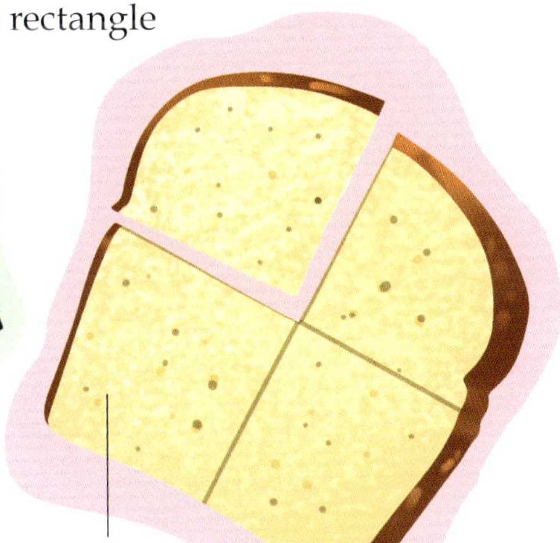

A quarter of a sandwich

A quarter of a banana

DID YOU KNOW?

A quarter is also called a 'fourth' since a quarter is one part out of four.

4. Activity: Fractions with Building Blocks

Build these fractions using building blocks.

You need: Blue and red building blocks, or any two colours of blocks.

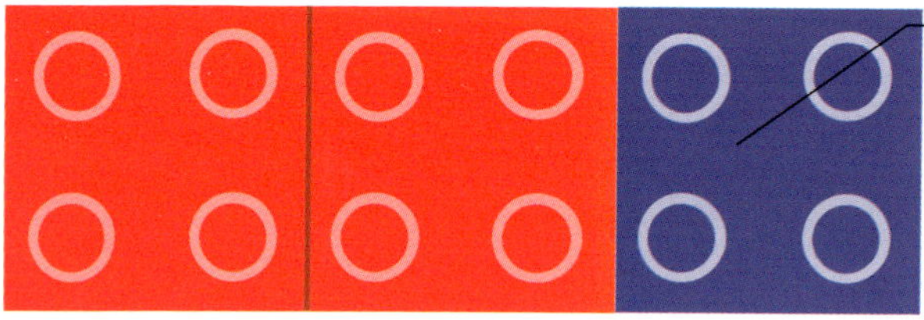

Place 2 red blocks and 1 blue block side by side. The blue block is 1 of 3 blocks. The fraction for it is **1/3 or one-third.**

Place blocks as shown here to build more fractions.

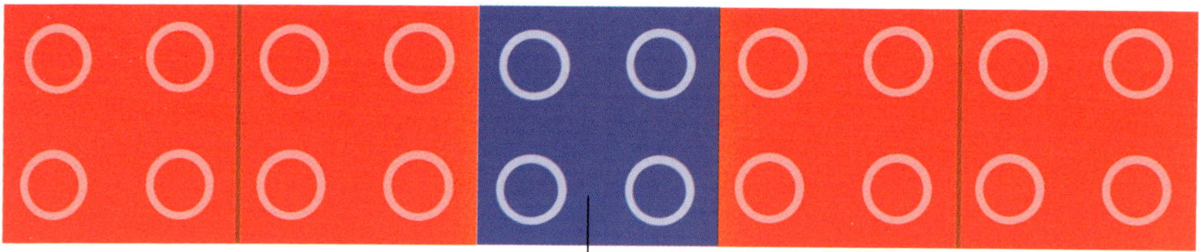

1/5
one-fifth

1/2
one-half

POCKET FACT

The blue block represents the numerator while the total of red and blue blocks is the denominator.

Quiz

If you use 1 blue block and 9 red blocks, what fraction represents the blue block?

Hint: There is 1 blue out of a total of ten blocks.

Answer: One-tenth (1/10)

Fraction Wall

This wall contains all fractions of a whole from halves to tenths.

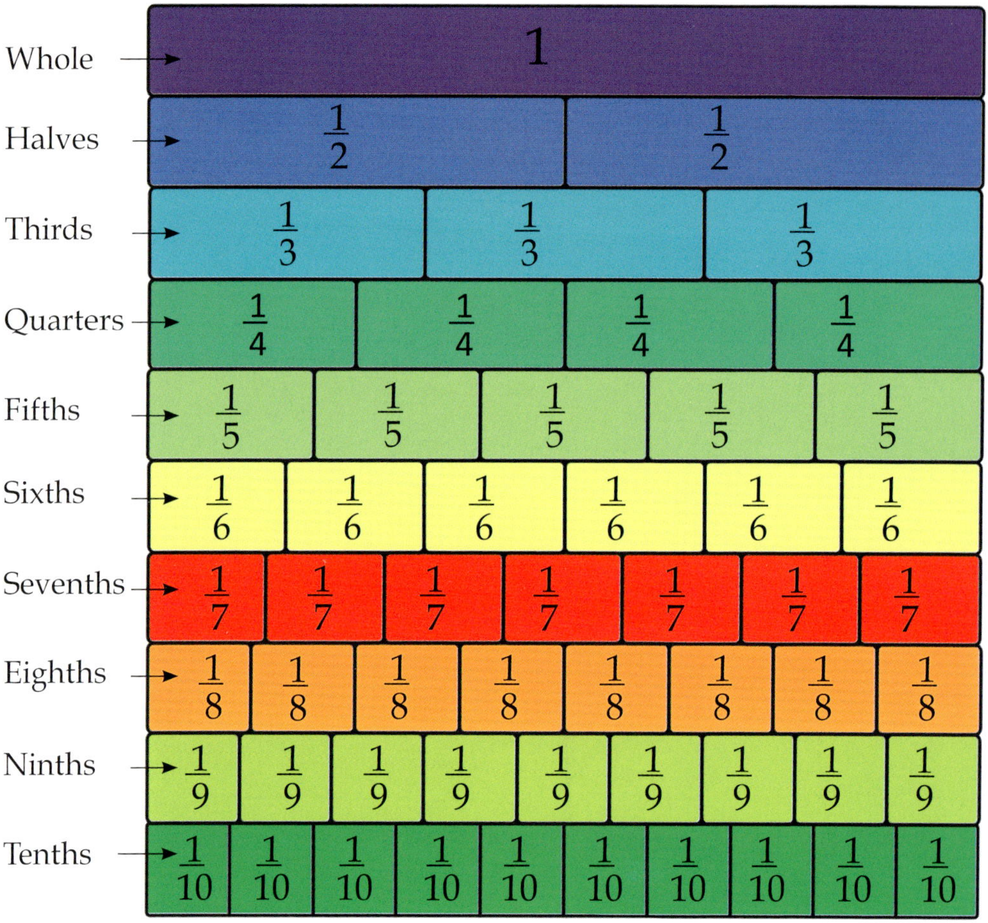

POCKET FACT

The fraction name depends on the total number of parts.

5. Let's Do Some More Counting

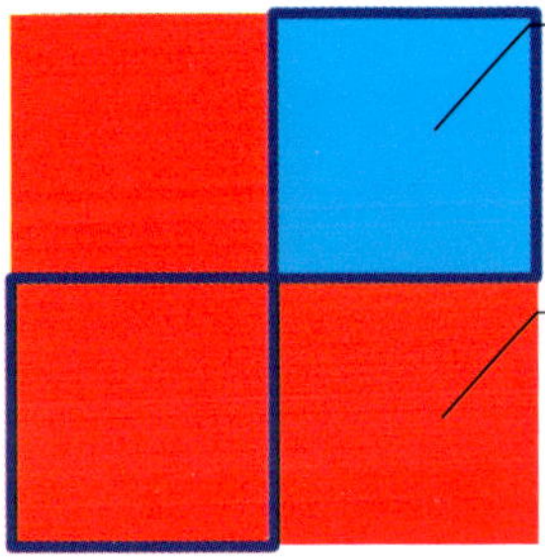

1 out of 4 pieces of the square is blue

3 out of 4 pieces of the square are red

So, 1/4 of the square is blue and 3/4 of the square is red.

Total number of pieces are 6.

Number of blue pieces is 1. So, 1/6 of the hexagon is blue.

Number of red pieces are 5. So, 5/6 of the hexagon is red.

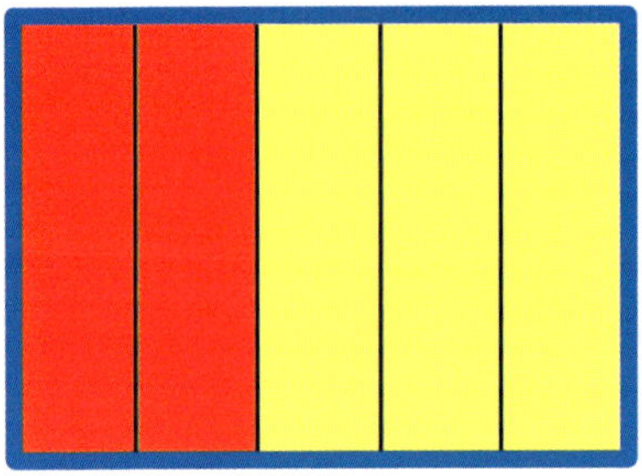

Total number of pieces is 5.

Number of **red** pieces is 2. So, **2/5** of the rectangle is **red**.

Number of **yellow** pieces is 3. So, **3/5** of the rectangle is **yellow**.

Total number of pieces is 6.

Number of blue pieces is 1. So, **1/6** of the rectangle is **blue**.

Number of orange pieces is 3. So, **3/6** of the rectangle is **orange**.

Number of pink pieces is 2. So, **2/6** of the rectangle is **pink**.

Quiz

Tim, Nancy and Coco were having pizza. Can you tell what fraction of pizza each of them has left on their plate?

Answer: (i) 3/6; (ii) 2/3; (iii) 3/4

Whole again

Six friends went out for a pizza party. They ordered a large pizza. They were each served a slice of pizza individually. How do they find out if they got the whole pizza as ordered or not?

They put their slices together.

These are 6 pieces out of 6, which is 6/6. They form one whole pizza. So, 6/6 is the same as 1!

In other words, 1/6 + 1/6 + 1/6 + 1/6 + 1/6 + 1/6 = 6/6

Quiz

How much should be added to 1/6 to make it same as 1?

Answer: 1/6 + 5/6 = 6/6; and 6/6=1

6. Mixed Numbers

Ana and Mario made 3 sandwiches and shared it equally among themselves. Each ate one whole sandwich and a half sandwich. Let's count how many each ate.

Each ate **one and a half** sandwiches.

One and a half is written like this:

Mixed numbers are used to count whole things and parts of things at the same time. A mixed number has both a whole number and a proper fraction combined into a **Mixed** number.

DID YOU KNOW?

Mixed Numbers are also called Mixed Fractions.

Check out these Mixed Numbers.

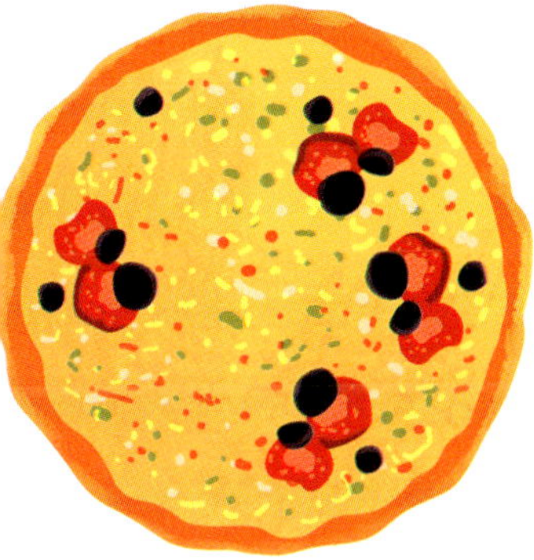

$1\frac{3}{4}$ pizza pieces

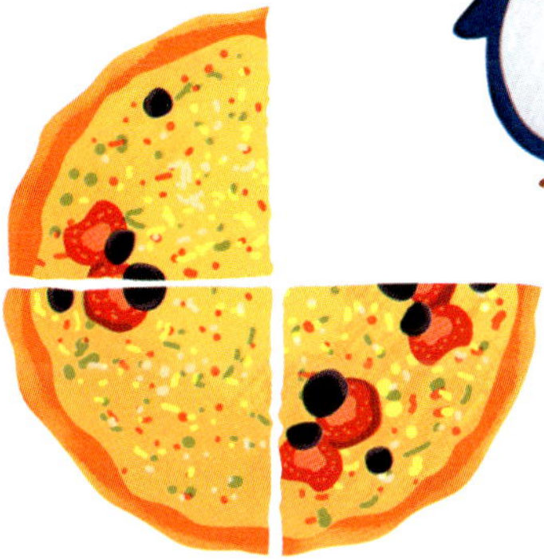

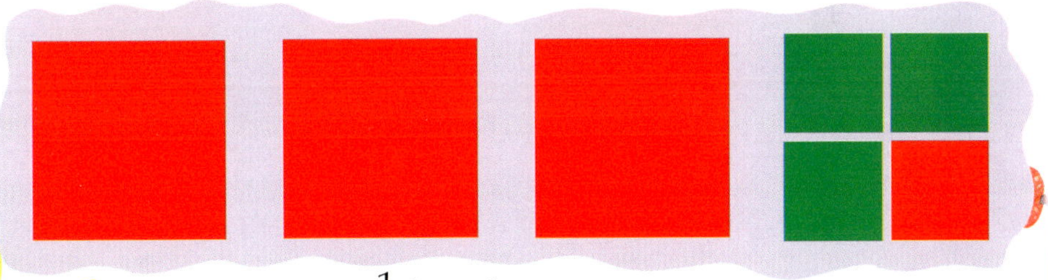

$3\frac{1}{4}$ red squares

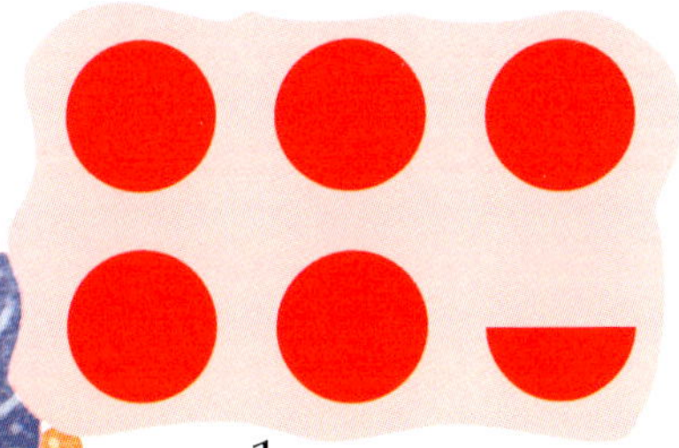

$5\frac{1}{2}$ circles

$4\frac{1}{2}$ glasses of water

Quiz

How will you write the mixed number six and a quarter?

Answer: A quarter is $\frac{1}{4}$. So, six and a quarter is $6\frac{1}{4}$.

7. Equivalent Fractions

These two circles appear to be divided into different number of parts.

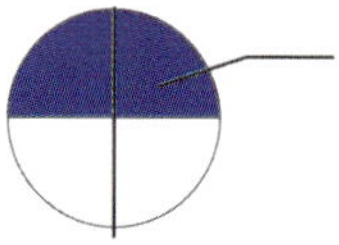

This circle has 2/4 blue parts

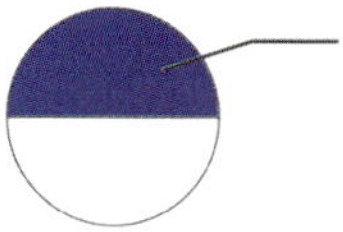

This circle has 1/2 blue parts

However, both circles have the same amount of blue. This means that 2/4 must be the same value as 1/2.

These two rectangles have different fractions in green.

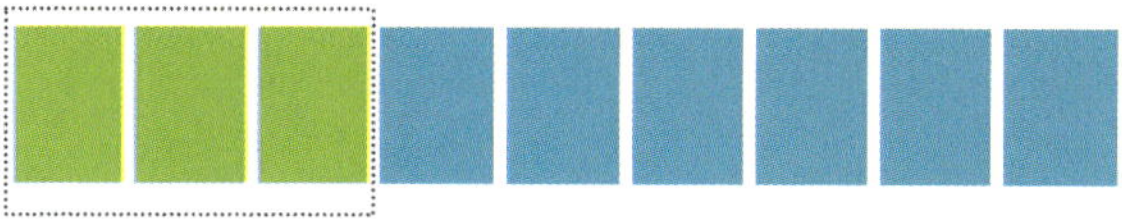

3/9 is green

1/3 is green

Even though the fractions look different, the same amount is green in both rectangles.

So, 1/3 = 3/9

POCKET FACT

Equivalent fractions have the same value, although they may have different numbers and appear different.

These fractions are equivalent, even though the whole is split into different number of parts.

1/3

2/6

4/12

Equivalent fractions in pizza slices

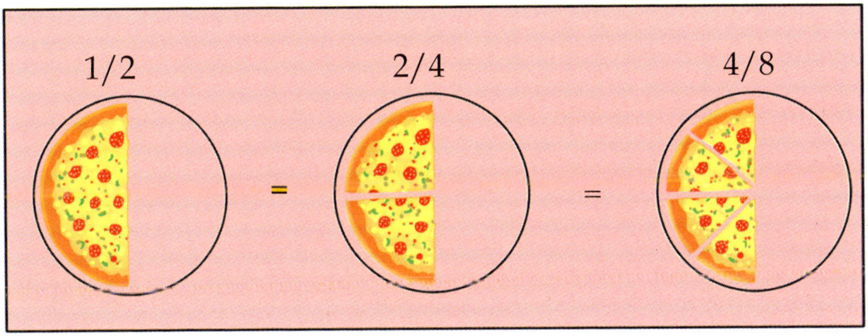

Making Equivalent Fractions

Multiply both numerator and denominator by the same number to get equivalent fractions.

$$\frac{1}{3} \xrightarrow{\times 2} \frac{2}{6} \xrightarrow{\times 2} \frac{4}{12}$$

$$\frac{1}{3} = \frac{2}{6} = \frac{4}{12}$$

Divide both numerator and denominator by the same number to get equivalent fractions.

$$\frac{10}{20} \xrightarrow{\div 5} \frac{2}{4} \xrightarrow{\div 2} \frac{1}{2}$$

$$\frac{10}{20} = \frac{2}{4} = \frac{1}{2}$$

If you keep dividing until you cannot divide any further, you have simplified the fraction.

Quiz

Simplify the fraction 3/6. (Hint: Divide by 3)

Answer: 3/6 = 1/2

When the numerator is the same as the denominator, then the fraction has the same equivalent value as 1. This is because when we divide a number by itself, the result is always '1'.

÷6

$$\frac{6}{6} = \frac{1}{1} = 1$$

÷6

÷10

$$\frac{10}{10} = \frac{1}{1} = 1$$

÷10

These fractions have different numbers, but the same equivalent value as '1'.

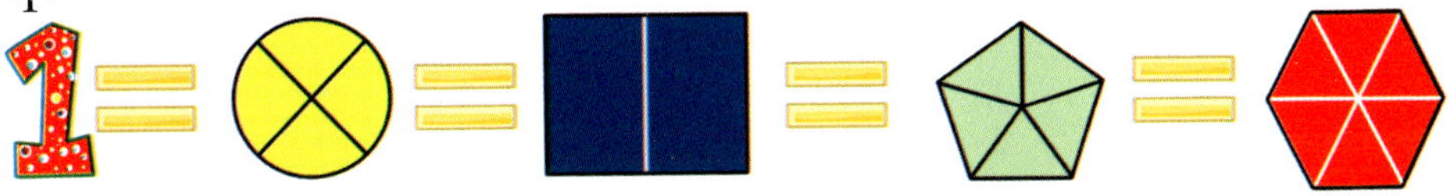

4/4 2/2 5/5 6/6

POCKET FACT

Only multiply or divide, never add or subtract, to get an equivalent fraction.

8. Activity: Equivalent Fractions

Multiply both numerator and denominator by the same number to get equivalent fractions.

You need:

- 5 strips of different coloured construction paper
- Markers
- Ruler

Step 1. Take 3-inch strips length-wise of five different coloured pieces of paper. All strips should have the same length.	
Step 2. Write '1 Whole 1/1' on one strip with a marker.	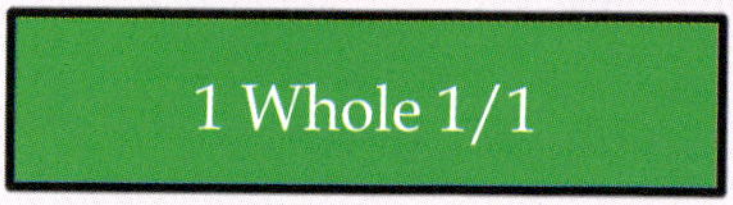
Step 3. Take another strip. Fold and cut in half. Write 1/2 on each half. Place it below the first strip. Note, the two halves make a whole.	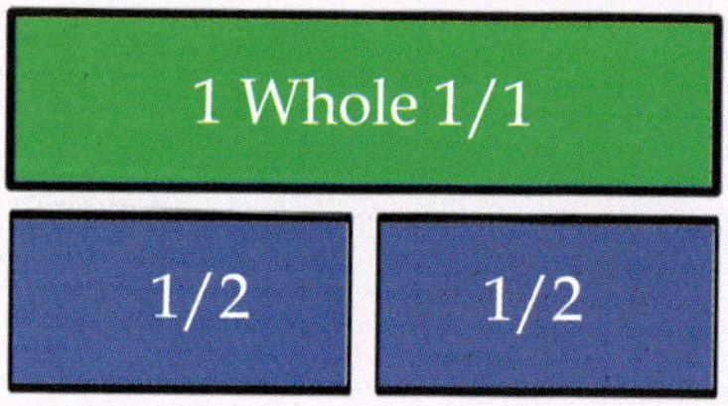

Step 4 Fold the next strip four times and cut. Write 1/4 on each part. Place it below the second strip. Four quarters are the same as two halves.

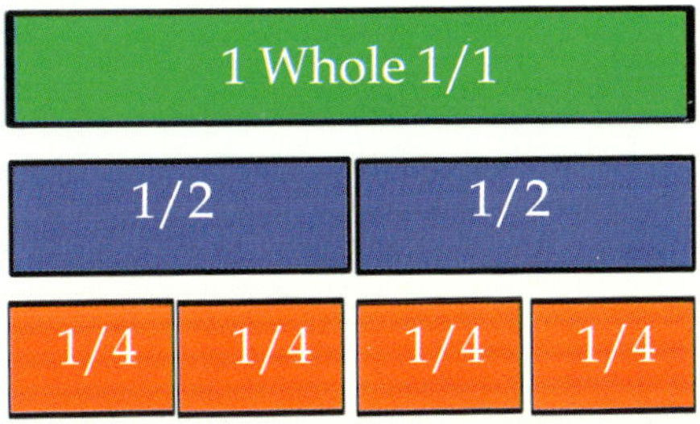

Step 5. Similarly cut the remaining two strips and write down 1/8 and 1/16 on them and place them below other sheets as shown. You now have a fraction wall of equivalent fractions.

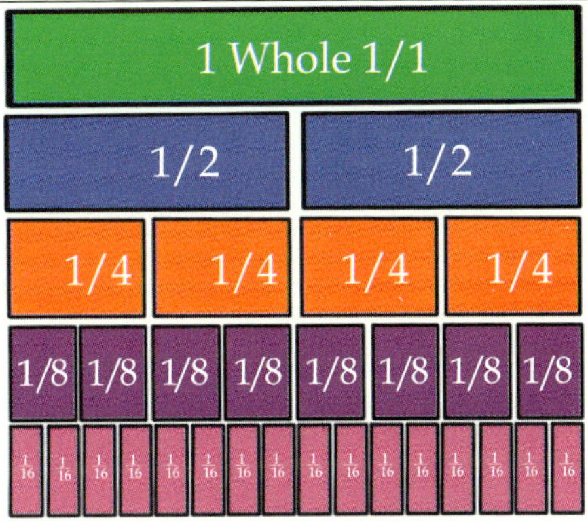

Quiz

If you cut another strip to place under 1/16, what fraction would you write?

Hint: Find out how many pieces you would cut.

Answer: 1/32

Equal Shares

To reach the big carrot on the other side, the rabbit has to follow the path that has shapes divided into equal shares. Can you help him?

Halves and Quarters

These three friends are working to find out halves and quarters correctly. Tick the correct answer.

1.

2.

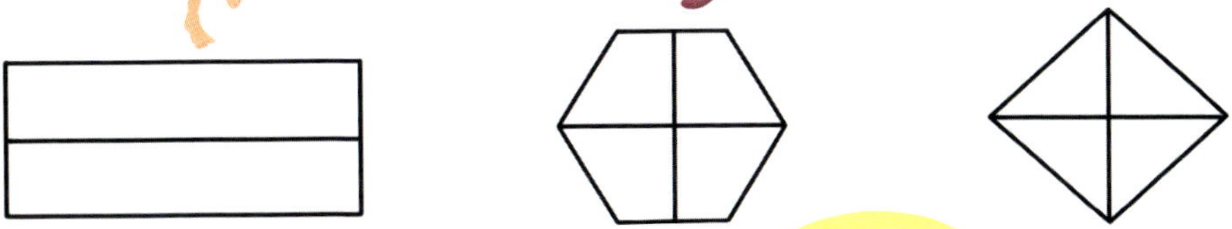

Mixed Numbers

Match the mixed number with the correct picture.

1.	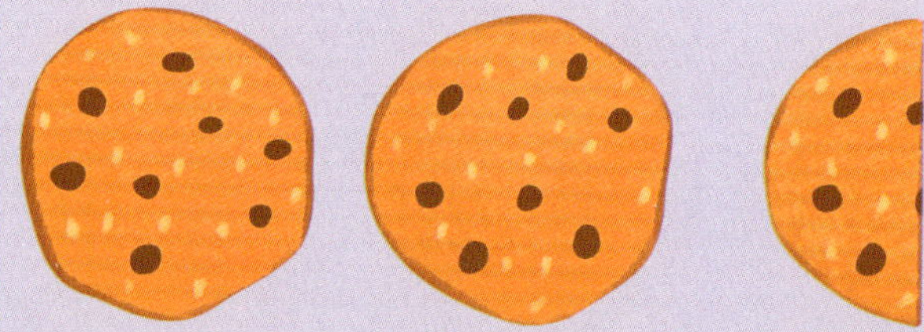	$1\,^1/_4$
2.		$2\,^1/_2$
3.	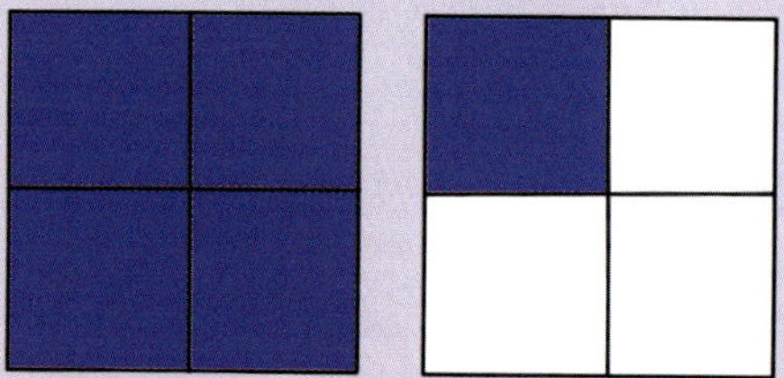	$1\,^1/_2$
4.		$3\,^6/_7$
5.	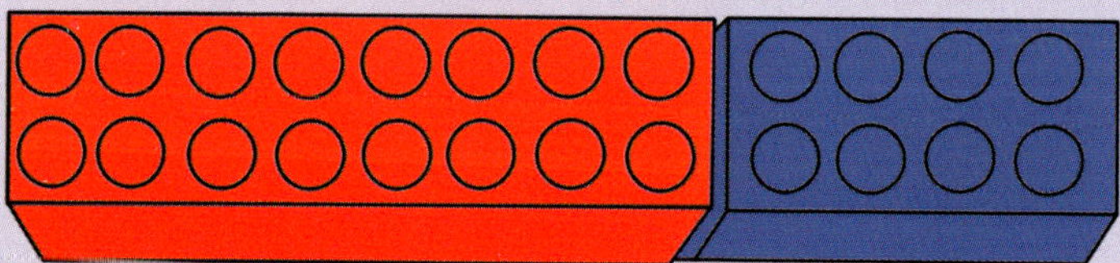	$4\,^1/_2$

Mixed Numbers

Circle all the equivalent fractions of 1/2 .

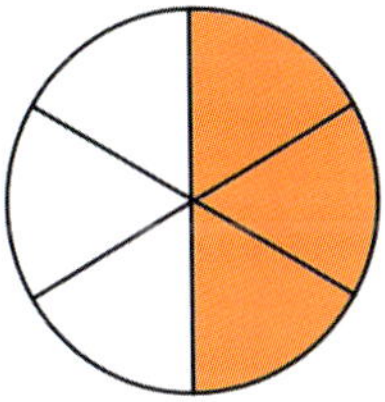
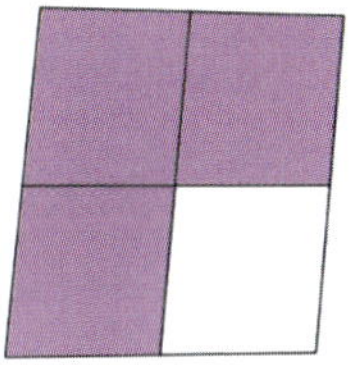
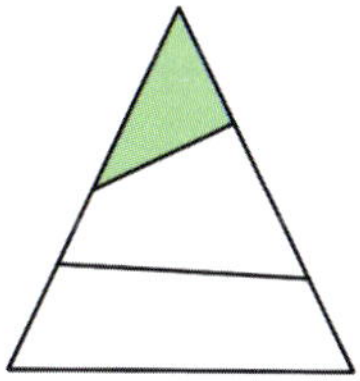

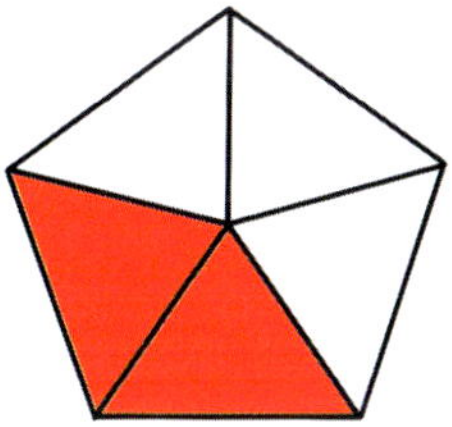

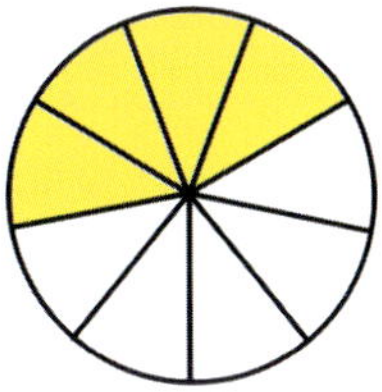

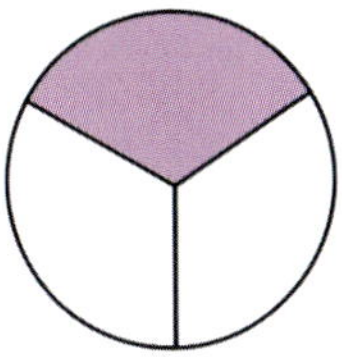
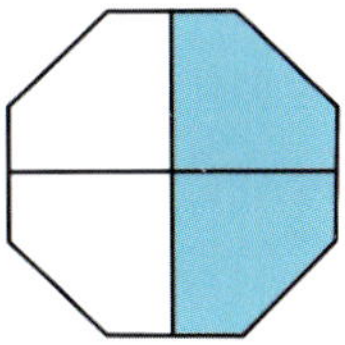

GLOSSARY

Add	to bring two or more numbers (or things) together to make a new total
Building blocks	a child's wooden or plastic toy brick
Divide	separate or be separated into parts
Equal	being the same in quantity, size, degree, or value
Equivalent	equal in value, amount, function, meaning, etc.
Mixed	composed of different varieties of the same thing
Multiply	increase or cause to increase greatly in number or quantity
Represent	depict
Share	a part or portion of a larger amount
Slice	a portion or share of something
Subtract	take away a number from another to calculate the difference
Value	the material or monetary worth of something

ANSWERS

Page 29.
(1) Roger
(2) Nancy

Page 30.
(1) $2\frac{1}{2}$ cookies
(2) $3\frac{6}{7}$ pies
(3) $1\frac{1}{4}$ green squares
(4) $4\frac{1}{2}$ hearts
(5) $1\frac{1}{2}$ blocks

Page 31.

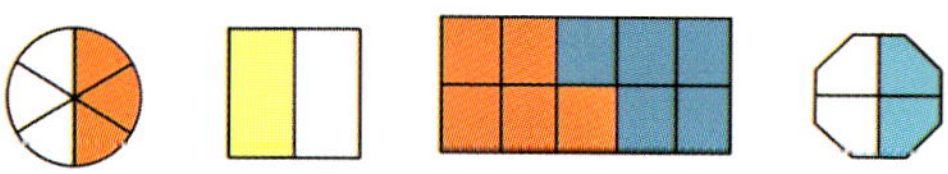